THE YOUR MOM SERIES
by Dicky Dates
YOUR MOM FINDS THE PERFECT WIENER
A Totally Innocent Children's Book for Adults with Dirty Minds
Premium Wiener Fuel
Certified Good Wiener

This book is a work of nonfiction. Names, identifying details, and circumstances have been altered where appropriate.

Printed in the United States of America

Florida Keys, Florida

Dedicated to:

Your Mom

Your Mom spent years looking for the perfect wiener.

Your Mom studied pictures of wieners for hours.

Some wieners were cute.

Some were weird.

Your Mom swiped through

hundreds of wieners.

She wanted a wiener that felt

just right in her hands.

Your Mom looked at every size.

Short Wieners.

Fat wieners.

Long wieners.

Some were just . . .

too much wiener for Your Mom.

She even asked her friends
which wiener they liked best.

Your Mom sighed.

Wieners are just so hard.

One day she spotted a very
unusual wiener.

This wiener only had one eye

and he always wore
protection.

He curved slightly to the left
when moving quickly.

When Your Mom held him, she knew he was the perfect wiener.

Just touching him was overwhelming

and made Your Mom very wet.

Your Mom played with her
wiener every day.

Petting her wiener
made him very happy.

Your Mom's wiener stood so proud and tall.

He dove into Your Mom's legs for extra love.

Your Mom's wiener was a dirty boy sometimes.

Nothing a moist rub down
couldn't fix!

After all the activity, Your Mom snuggled her favorite wiener.

Does Your Mom have a perfect wiener?

Please Share!

Tag and collaborate with @dickydates and @yourmomseries

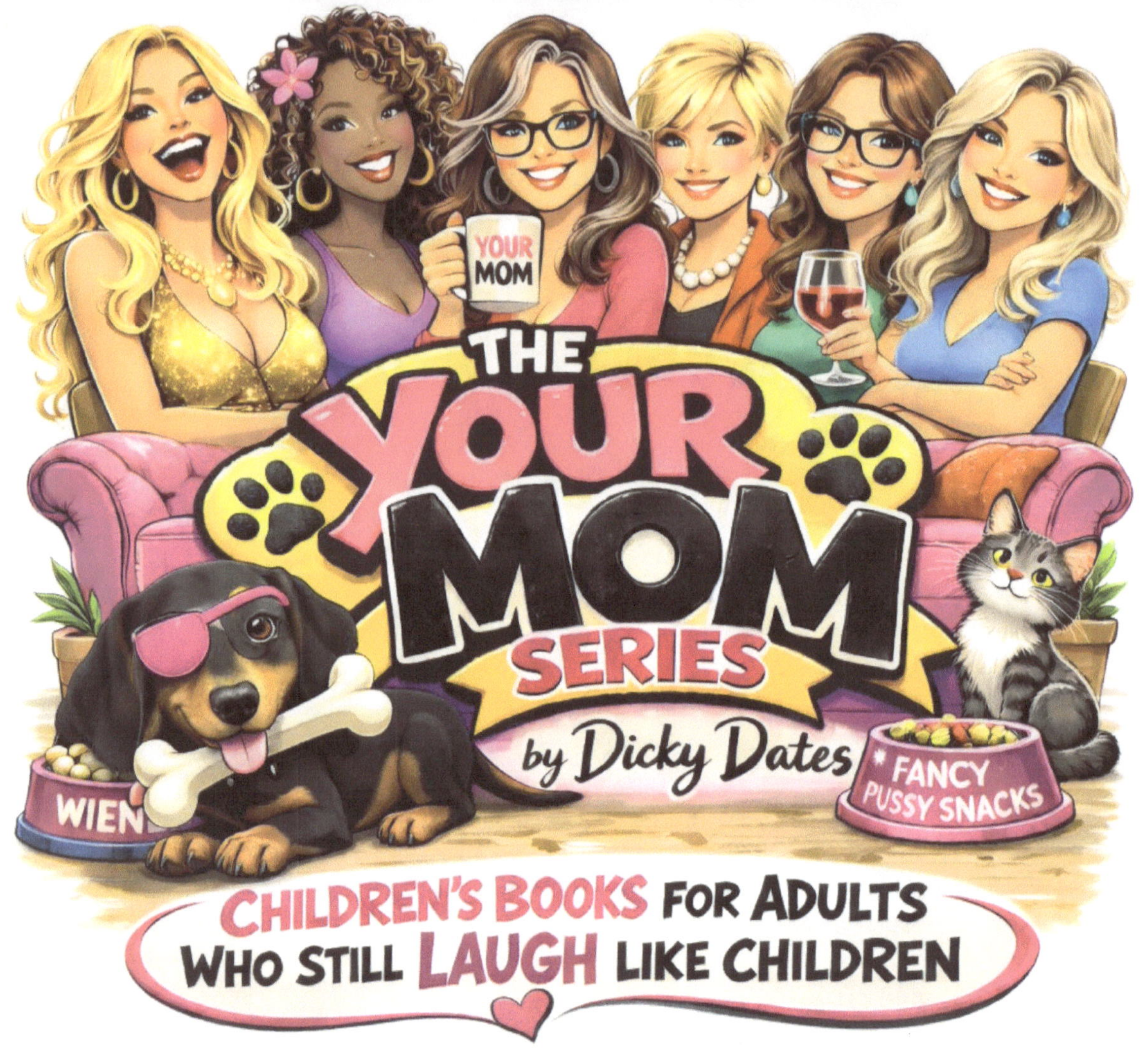

Stay updated on new books and merchandise!

www.dickydates.com

What innocence will Your Mom encounter next?